Sous Vide Vegetarian Cookbook

Easy Vegeterian Meals for the Sophisticated Palette

Michelle Jones

resulting actions solely under their purview. There are no scenarios in which the publisher or the original author of this work can be in any fashion deemed liable for any hardship or damages that may befall them after undertaking information described herein.

Additionally, the information found on the following pages is intended for informational purposes only and should thus be considered, universal. As befitting its nature, the information presented is without assurance regarding its continued validity or interim quality. Trademarks that are mentioned are done without written consent and can in no way be considered an endorsement from the trademark holder.

Table of Contents

Introduction

Congratulations on downloading this book and thank you for doing so.

The following chapters will discuss the sous vide cooking method and how you are able to use it even while following the vegetarian diet. Many of the best-known recipes that are used with sous vide are great meat choices, but for those who are following the vegetarian diet, you aren't singled out. Sous vide works well with other dishes, including vegetables, so you can stick with your diet and get all of the benefits of using this great cooking method.

This book is going to give you all the resources that you need to get started on the sous vide cooking method as a vegetarian. We will start out with some basics of the vegetarian diet for those who have never followed it before and then we will move on to some of the basics that come with sous vide cooking. When that is done, the rest of the book will focus on some of the best vegetarian sous vide recipes so you can give this cooking method a try while sticking with your healthy diet.

When you are following the vegetarian diet, you may hear about sous vide and assume that this is not a cooking method that you can use. But with the help of the great recipes that are in this book, you will be able to enjoy this cooking method while enjoying some good vegetarian classics.

There are plenty of books on this subject on the market, thanks again for choosing this one! Every effort was made to ensure it is full of as much useful information as possible, please enjoy!

Chapter 1: The Basics of the Vegetarian Diet

While there are a lot of stereotypes that come with the vegetarian diet, there is actually a lot of complexity to choosing a meat-free diet like this one. There are people of all kinds of backgrounds and ages that choose to be vegetarian. Some may do so because they think that it is inhumane to eat living things. Some do it because they want to live a healthier lifestyle. And others may not even like the taste of meat so they go with this option.

Those who are on the vegetarian diet are never going to eat meat, poultry, or fish. Rather than relying on these sources of food like other Americans might, they will rely on plant-based foods and grains in order to get their nutrition and to make their meals.

Types of vegetarians

What a lot of non-vegetarians may not realize is that there are actually few different types of vegetarians. Some will choose to avoid meat products like beef, fish, and poultry, but they will allow themselves to eat eggs, milk, and cheese. There are others, who are more commonly called vegans, who will avoid eating any product that comes from an animal.

For example, a lacto-ovo-vegetarian will eat things like seeds, nuts, beans, vegetables, fruits, grains, eggs, dairy foods, and milk, but they are going to avoid eating poultry, fish, and meat. Those who are considered Lacto-vegetarians will follow a similar diet, but they will avoid eating eggs from any animal. Then there are the vegans, those who will stay away from any type of animal based product, such as meat, dairy and milk products, gelatin, lard, and any other foods that come from animal sources. There are even some vegans who will choose to not eat honey.

As you can see, there are a lot of ways that someone can choose to be a vegetarian. All of them are going to avoid meat products so this is the most important thing to remember, but whether they just avoid meat or if they avoid all products that come from an animal source will vary based on the type of vegetarian they are.

Why would people become vegetarian?

The next question that you may have is why do people choose to follow a vegetarian diet? There are a lot of reasons that people will choose to go on this kind of diet. Some have a personal preference for avoiding meat, such as worrying about inhumane treatment of animals. Others have health concerns that make it healthier for them to rely on a plant based diet. There are even some people who don't like to eat meat at all so they will stick with eating fruits and vegetables. Many people go on this kind of diet because they believe it is healthier and will help them to lose weight.

It is common for many vegetarians to go with this kind of diet because of ethical reasons. For example, many times the person who follows this diet will do so because they don't want to see animals killed or harm. They may have some big objections to the way that animals are raised or treated on farms.

Another concern that is often voiced is about the environment. There are some issues that have been cited about how animals and the farms they live on can affect different aspects of the environment. For example, the animal waste from these farms can pollute the land and water, or there are forests that are cut down so that the grazing cattle will have room to graze.

In some cases, there are religious beliefs that will play a part in whether someone becomes a vegetarian or not. Those who follow the religion of Jainism will practice nonviolence, and they will not eat meat, along with certain vegetables like garlic, potatoes, and onions. Hindus also don't believe in eating meat and they are one of the largest vegetarian populations. They believe in having self-control and control of their own spirits and mind. Some will eat fish, but they will avoid other types of meats to follow this religion.

There are a lot of people who have been attracted to the vegetarian diet because of all the health benefits.

They may want to reduce some of their health risks that come from eating a meat based diet, or they want to be able to lose weight while still getting all of the nutrients that they need, and the vegetarian diet is one of the best ways to do this. Whether they go on this kind of diet for the short term to help them get healthier eating habits to lose weight or a more permanent change, vegetarianism can really help out with both options.

There are a lot of reasons that people will choose to go with a vegetarian diet and picking out the reason that works the best for you will help you determine whether this is the right diet plan for you.

What do I eat on the vegetarian diet?

Following the vegetarian diet is actually pretty simple. When you are picking out your meals, you need to make sure that you avoid some foods like poultry, fish, and other sources of meat. But there are still so many different options that you can choose from that are vegetarian approved, can fill you up with lots of nutrients, and taste so good. Some of the foods that you are able to eat on the vegetarian diet includes:

- Fruits and vegetables: Fresh produce is going to become one of the main parts of all your meals. Full of healthy vitamins and minerals, these will help you stay strong, fill you up quickly, and are low in calories. Make sure that you go for fresh or frozen options. Canned are going to be packed in sugars so they are not the best option for you.

- Grains: Grains are a good way to fill up your meals, but make sure that you pick out the right grains. White and processed grains are basically going to turn into sugars in your body after you eat them. Whole grains are the best options so try to stick with those in as much as possible.

- Dairy products: Dairy products are another good source of nutrients. Most have high levels of protein inside of them, as well as calcium and other vitamins that the body needs. Add a few servings of these into your day and you will get a lot of nutrients all at once.

- Eggs: Vegetarians can eat egg products, so these are great options when it comes to making a quick dinner or a good breakfast in the morning. These have a lot of the protein and other nutrients that you may be missing from other sources of meat; so, they are a good idea to add into your diet plan.

In addition to avoiding meat products, you should also avoid sugars and sweets on this diet plan. It is not expressly forbidden and you can have them on occasion, but if you are going on this kind of diet plan for the health benefits, and most people who choose this diet do go on it for those benefits, you will want to cut out these unhealthy foods as well.

How is the vegan diet different?

Another question that some people who are new to the vegetarian diet may have is how the vegetarian diet is different from the vegan diet. The vegetarian diet is one where the followers are going to abstain from fish, poultry, and other meat products. They will have to find their sources of protein from other places, but they are able to eat other types of foods.

On the other hand, a vegan is going to take it a bit further. In addition to avoiding animal meat like beef, poultry, and fish, they are also going to avoid products that come from animals. This would include milk, dairy products, eggs, and even honey in some cases. They believe that any product that comes from animals is not good to eat and so they will avoid all of these.

Of course, the vegan diet is going to be a bit more difficult to follow and you do need to make sure that you are careful with the nutrients that you get. When you cut out this much food, you have to watch that you are getting the right nutrients so your body is not deprived. It is still possible to follow a vegan diet and be healthy, you will just need to be more health conscious in the process.

Things to consider on the vegetarian diet

Since you are cutting out a major source of food, mostly the meat category that contains the protein that our bodies need to stay healthy, it is important that vegetarians work to ensure that they get the right nutrients. It is easy to eat too much of one type of food and not get all of the nutrients that the body needs to stay healthy.

The first thing that you should consider is finding the right protein source. There are some options that are available, you just need to make sure that you are getting enough of them in your diet. If you are still following the vegetarian diet that will allow you to eat eggs and dairy products, make sure to enjoy those as they can be good sources of protein that allow you to stay on the vegetarian diet. Tofu is another great option with lots of protein as well.

While fruits and vegetables are healthy for you, it is best if you take your time to eat a wide variety of this product. Eating the same few options all of the time is going to make you lack some of the nutrients that you need and can make the diet a little bit boring to follow. Plan out your meals ahead of time so you are eating a lot of different fruits and vegetables. This changes up the nutrients that you enjoy and will make it easier to stay healthy with lots of nutrients along the way.

Health benefits

A big reason that people like to switch over to the vegetarian diet is that of all the health benefits that they are able to realize. The eating patterns that have come with vegetarianism are associated with so many health benefits such as lower blood pressure, a reduction in heart disease risk, lower obesity levels and so much more.

In addition, vegetarians often end up consuming a lower number of calories from fat, as well as fewer calories overall in their diet, while still getting a ton more nutrients in their diet including vitamin C, potassium, and fiber compared to those who are not on this diet plan. When these characteristics, as well as some new lifestyle factors that are often added to the diet plan, are put together, it is no wonder that the vegetarian diet can be so healthy to follow.

There are so many reasons that people will choose to go on the vegetarian diet. They want to lose weight, they want to stop cruelty to animals, or they are following the rules of their religion. No matter the reasons, a vegetarian diet can be just the answer that you are looking for to improve your overall health and get the good nutrients that you need.

Chapter 2: What Is Sous Vide?

There are many different types of cooking methods that you can choose to work with. You can bake casseroles, cakes, and baked goods. You can choose to grill some of your favorite meats. You can use the slow cooker in order to get a meal ready by the time you make it back home. All of these cooking methods have been in use for a long time, but none provide quite the good taste or ease of use as working with sous vide.

Sous vide is French for under vacuum. And this is a good description of how you would complete this cooking method. You will start by creating a warm water bath and heating it up to whatever temperature you would like your food to reach when it is done cooking. While that is heating up, you will prepare the food, cutting, dicing, and so on, that you want to use and then throw it all into a food safe bag.

This bag will then need to be thrown into the water bath and it will cook up until the foods are all done. Depending on the type of food that you are working with, it can take a few hours or sometimes you can put the food in during the morning and have dinner ready when you come home.

The best thing about using this method is that the food will taste amazing no matter how high your culinary skills are when you get started. Many people like to use this method to cook up different cuts of meat because they will come out perfectly each time. Whether you are working with an expensive cut of meat that is easy to ruin or you want to take a tough cut of meat and make it edible, the sous vide method is the right one for you.

Of course, you don't have to eat just meat with this option, as you will see with some of the great meals that we will provide later in this book. You can also choose to cook up desserts, vegetables, and so much more. Sous vide is such a versatile option for cooking that you are sure to see so many recipes that you know and love while following this cooking method and when you combine it with the vegetarian diet, you are also going to end up with some healthy meal solutions at the same time.

Another thing that is so great about the sous vide cooking method is that it is simple. Each meal will have a cooking time that you should stick with as a minimum to make sure that the food is cooked correctly, but you can leave the food in for longer time, which is something that is just not found with other cooking methods. If you are running late, need to leave the dish in while you are at work, or you get distracted and forget, you don't have to worry about it. Your food will not become overcooked when you use a sous vide water bath, making it the perfect addition to any kitchen.

Benefits of sous vide cooking

There are a lot of benefits that come with choosing to cook with sous vide water bath. It is considered one of the easiest cooking methods to use and it can make your food taste so amazing when you are done. It is easy enough for even beginner chefs to work with, so you won't have to worry about exact times or other concerns like you do with some alternative cooking methods. Some of the benefits that you can enjoy when it comes to cooking with sous vide include:

- Works with many foods: While you may have heard about sous vide in the past and how it works with meat dishes, there are actually a lot of foods that do well with sous vide. You can use it to help with vegetables, grain dishes, and even with desserts!
- Can leave in longer: While there is a minimum amount of time that the food should stay in the water, there is no maximum time. If the meal needs to be pushed back until later or you need to put it in and not get to it until you get off work; that is just fine. With sous vide, the food will never cook higher than the temperature in the water bath, so you can leave it in the machine for as long as you would like without worrying about overheating or overcooking.
- Easy to set up: Setting up the water bath is pretty easy. Most sous vide baths will come with the container that you need to use. You just need to fill it up and then set the

thermometer to the temperature that you want. Once the water bath is warm, you can add the food and it will cook up properly. And that is all that you need to do to make this cooking method work!

- Cost effective: In the beginning, sous vide was kind of expensive. There weren't a lot of people who were using sous vide because it was only available in commercial kitchens. But the more people became interested in this cooking method, many companies have started to make machines that are affordable and have many options. It is easy to purchase a sous vide water bath, making it easy to use this method in your own kitchen.

As you can see, there are a lot of great reasons to work with sous vide cooking. It is fast, effective, and will cook your food the way that you would like. With just one time trying out this machine, and you will want to start cooking all your meals, even your vegetarian meals, using this cooking method.

Food safety

There are a few things that you are able to do to make sure that you are maintaining food safety when you are using the sous vide method. This is an extremely effective method of making your meals, but there are some things that you can do to make sure that your food stays safe.

The first thing to remember is that you should never reuse bags. You do not want to cause cross contamination between different foods because you were using the same bags over and over again. Some people think this is a good way to save money, but there are a number of issues. Not only are you dealing with the issue of cross-contamination, you are also dealing with something being wrong with the bag, such as getting a hole in it, and the food not cooking properly.

In addition, you should make sure that the air is completely out of the bag before you place it into the water. If there is air inside the bag, it prevents the water from getting right on the food and can mess with the cooking times and the food that you are working with. Always make sure that you remove all of the air from the bag, vacuum sealing is the best way to do this, and then let the water get to the proper temperature before you even add the bag in so your food cooks properly.

Proper cooking of your food is so important. You do not want to take the food out of the water early or it may not be cooked all of the ways through. It is fine to leave the food in the water bath a little bit longer if you would like, but you should make sure that you don't take it out early because your food won't be at the right temperatures.

Chapter 3: Soups to Fill You Up

Butternut Squash Soup

Ingredients:
- Pepper (.5 tsp.)
- Salt (.5 tsp.)
- Canned coconut milk (.75 c.)
- Chicken broth (2 c.)
- Minced garlic cloves (2)
- Diced onion (1)
- Butter (2 Tbsp.)
- Minced Thai chilies (2)
- Cubed butternut squash (4 c.)

Preparations:
1. Bring out your sous vide machine and fill it up properly with water. Set the water bath to 183 degrees.
2. Place both the chilies and butternut squash in a food safe bag and seal it shut so all of the air is out of the bag.
3. Place this bag of food into the water bath and cook this for 90 minutes.
4. When the cooking time is done, melt the butter in a skillet with the garlic and the onion so that they become caramelized.
5. Remove the squash from the water bath and pour it into a blender. Add the rest of your ingredients as well.
6. Blend this on a high setting until it is the right consistency that you want. Add a bit of water to help make it thinner if you would like. Serve this chilled or hot.

Apple and Pumpkin Soup

Ingredients:
- Pepper (.5 tsp.)
- Salt (.5 tsp.)
- Vegetable broth (3.5 c.)
- Minced garlic cloves (2)
- Diced sweet onion (1)
- Butter (2 Tbsp.)
- Peeled and diced apples (2)
- Cubed pumpkins (3 c.)
- Cashews (.3 c.)

Preparations:
1. Bring out your sous vide machine and fill it up with water. Let the water bath heat up to 183 degrees.
2. Place both the apples and the pumpkin into a food safe bag and then seal it shut properly. Put this bag inside of the water bath and let these cook for 90 minutes.
3. When the cooking time is almost done, melt some butter in a skillet and then cook the garlic and onion and let these two caramelize.
4. Now you can take the pumpkin and apples out of the water bath and pour into a blender. Add the pepper, salt, vegetable broth, garlic, and onion to the blender as well.
5. Blend this on a high setting until it is smooth. If you would like a soup that is thinner, add some more chicken broth or water.
6. Ladle this into some bowls and enjoy when ready.

Asian Vegetable Soup

Ingredients:

- Bay leaf (1)
- Water (5.5 c.)
- Butter (2 Tbsp.)
- Diced sweet potatoes (.75 lb.)
- Diced carrots (1 c.)
- Shredded spring onions (1 handful)
- Udon noodles (1.25 lbs.)
- Sake (1.5 Tbsp.)
- Japanese soy sauce (1 Tbsp.)
- Dried dill weed (.5 tsp.)
- Pepper
- Salt
- Minced garlic head (1)
- Minced shallots (1.5 c.)
- Bamboo shoots (.5 c.)
- Sliced Porcini mushrooms (1.25 lbs.)

Preparations:

1. To start, take out your sous vide machine and heat it up to 183 degrees.
2. While the water bath is heating up, take out a food safe bag and combine the carrots, butter, and sweet potatoes inside. Place into the water bath and cook for 55 minutes.
3. In a second food safe bag, combine the garlic, shallots, bamboo shoots, mushrooms, bay leaf, and water. Seal up this bag and cook for 43 minutes. Place to the side when done.

4. Turn your oven to 400 degrees. Take the sweet potatoes out of the bag when they are done and arrange half of them and the carrots on the baking pan.

5. Place into the oven. After 9 minutes, take the baking pan out of the oven and set to the side.

6. The remainder of the carrots and the sweet potatoes should be pureed in the food processor.

7. Place the prepared mushroom mixture into a big pot along with the pureed carrots and sweet potatoes. Season with the dill, pepper, and salt as the mixture comes to a boil.

8. Add the noodles, sake, and soy sauce.

9. When this is done boiling, pour into some serving bowls and garnish with the roasted sweet potatoes and carrots and the spring onions before serving.

Creamed Corn Soup

Ingredients:
- Heavy cream (.75 c.)
- Nutmeg
- Salt (1 tsp.)
- Olive oil (1.5 Tbsp.)
- Water (5.5 c.)
- Husked corn ears (4)
- Minced chives (4 Tbsp.)

Preparations:
1. Take out your sous vide machine and set the water bath to reach 183 degrees. While that is heating, cut the kernels off the corn.
2. Add some water and the corn cobs to a food safe bag and seal it up.
3. In another food safe bag, place the nutmeg, salt, olive oil, and corn kernels inside. Seal up this bag, making sure to get rid of as much air as possible and place into the fridge.
4. Place the bag with the corn cobs into the water bath and cook for two hours. At the last twenty-five minutes, add the other bag and let it cook.
5. When these are done, take the liquid from the bag with the corn kernels and add it to the pot, but keep the solids for now.
6. Fold in the cream and simmer for 13 minutes on a moderate heat.
7. Now strain out the liquid from your corn cobs and pour that into the pot. After stirring, add the rest of the ingredients and let these warm up before serving.

Pea Soup

Ingredients:
- Green peas (12 oz.)
- Parsnip (1)
- Chopped carrot (1)
- Minced garlic cloves (2)
- Chopped shallots (1 c.)
- Greek yogurt (4 tsp.)
- Fennel seeds (.5 tsp.)
- Dill weed (1 tsp.)
- Pepper
- Salt
- Water (1 c.)
- Vegetable stock (1 c.)

Preparations:
1. Take out the sous vide machine and fill it up with some water. Set the temperature so the water bath gets to 183 degrees.
2. Using a food safe bag, add the peas, parsnip, carrot, garlic, and shallots. Seal up the bag, make sure to get all the air out.
3. Place this bag of food into the water and let it cook for 55 minutes.
4. When the meal is done, take the bag out of the water bath and add these ingredients to a food processor.
5. Add the water, seasoning, and stock as well and puree everything. When this is done, pour into a container and leave in the fridge to chill.
6. Spoon this soup into individual bowls. Top each one with some Greek yogurt and enjoy.

Root Vegetable Soup

Ingredients:

- Rosemary sprig (1)
- Peeled garlic clove (2)
- Diced shallot (1)
- Diced celery stalk (1)
- Diced parsnip (1)
- Diced carrots (2)
- Water (1)
- Vegetable stock (5 c.)
- Pepper
- Salt
- Bay leaves (2)

Preparations:

1. Set up your sous vide machine by adding some water. Set the water bath to 183 degrees.
2. Each of your vegetables, once they have been prepared, should be placed inside their own food safe bag.
3. Divide the rest of the ingredients between these bags and then seal them all properly. Place into the hot water bath.
4. These bags need to cook for at least two hours. When they are done, strain out the liquid from the bags into a pot, but reserve the vegetables.
5. Let this simmer on a lower heat for about 10 minutes and then take the liquid off the heat.
6. At this time, place the vegetables into the pot. Using an immersion blender, blend everything together until they are nice and smooth and then serve warm.

Red Pepper Chowder

Ingredients:

- Salt
- Bay leaf (1)
- Smashed garlic clove (1)
- Chopped bell pepper (1)
- Chopped gold potato
- Olive oil (1 Tbsp.)
- Cauliflower florets (2 c.)
- Pepper
- Parmesan
- Warmed whole milk (1 c.)
- Vegetable broth (2 c.)
- Cumin (.25 tsp.)
- Coriander (.25 tsp.)

Preparations:

1. Take out the sous vide machine and fill it up with water. Set the temperature to reach 185 degrees.
2. While the sous vide machine heats up, combine the cumin, coriander, salt, bay leaf, garlic clove, olive oil, bell pepper, potato, and cauliflower in a food safe bag.
3. Seal up the bag and then add it to the water bath. Let the meal cook for about two hours.
4. When the vegetables are done, take the bag out of the water bath and then pour them out of the bag into a cooking pot.
5. Add the vegetable broth and milk into the pot and then use an immersion blender to blend these well.
6. Season with the pepper, salt, and Parmesan cheese before serving.

Beet Soup

Ingredients:

- Water (3 c.)
- Bay leaf (1)
- Chopped red beets (2 lbs.)
- Salt (.75 tsp.)
- Sliced leek (1)
- Diced onion (1)
- Caraway seeds (1.5 tsp.)
- Olive oils (1 Tbsp.)
- Dill
- Apple cider vinegar
- Whole milk yogurt (.5 c.)

Preparations:

1. Take out the sous vide machine and let the water bath heat up to 185 degrees.
2. Heat up some oil in a skillet and then add the caraway seeds when it begins simmering. Toss the seeds around so they start crackling.
3. Add some salt, the leek, and the onion and let these cook for a bit until the onion becomes tender.
4. Let this cool a bit while adding some salt, the bay leaf, and the beets into a bowl.
5. Stir this to combine and then divide it into two food safe bags. Seal up the bags properly.
6. Place your bags into the water bath and let them cook in there for 2 hours.
7. When the cooking time is up, take the bags out of the water and place all of the ingredients into a clean pot.

8. Add the water into this and then blend these ingredients with the help of an immersion blender. Stir the yogurt.

9. If you would like to thin out the soup a bit, just add some more liquid.

10. Season this with just a bit of the apple cider vinegar and then garnish with the dill before serving.

Sweet Potato Bisque

Ingredients:

- Butter (3 Tbsp.)
- Bay leaf (1)
- Minced garlic clove (1)
- Ginger (1 Tbsp.)
- Died leeks (1 c.)
- Sliced sweet potatoes (2)
- Pepper
- Sat
- Heavy cream (1 c.)
- Vegetable stock (1 c.)

Preparations:

1. Bring out your sous vide machine and fill it up with some water. Let the water bath heat up to 184 degrees.

2. Add the butter, garlic, ginger, leeks, and potatoes into a food safe bag and seal it up, making sure that the air is all out of the bag.

3. Place the bag of food into the water bath and let it cook for 90 minutes.

4. After this time, take the bag out and place all of the ingredients besides the bay leaf into a food blender. Add the pepper, salt, and heavy cream as well.

5. Process these ingredients until they are smooth. Pour into bowls and enjoy.

Chapter 4: Easy Salads as a Side or as a Meal

Green Bean and Potato Salad

Ingredients:
- Pepper (.5 tsp.)
- Salt (.5 tsp.)
- Honey (3 Tbsp.)
- Lemon juice (3 Tbsp.)
- Olive oil (.3 c.)
- Sliced green onions (6)
- Trimmed green beans (1 lb.)
- Quartered baby potatoes (2 lbs.)

Preparations:
1. Fill up your sous vide machine and set the water bath to 183 degrees.
2. Place your prepared potatoes into a food safe bag and seal it shut. In another bag, do the same with the green beans.
3. First, put the bag with the potatoes into the water bath and cook for 30 minutes. Once this time is up, add the green beans and cook for another hour.
4. When this time is done, take the vegetables out of the water bath, placing them in an ice water bath so they can chill.

5. Drain the potatoes out into a bowl and then drain the green beans, cut them in half and then place into the bowl with the onions.

6. To make the vinaigrette, whisk the pepper, salt, honey, lemon juice, and oil. Pour this on top of the salad and stir to coat it all.

7. Leave in the fridge until you want to serve.

Rainbow Veggie Bowl

Ingredients:
- Diced Roma tomatoes (2)
- Chili pepper (1)
- Sweet pepper (1)
- Sliced zucchini (2)
- Celery seeds (.5 tsp.)
- Hungarian paprika (1 tsp.)
- Pepper
- Salt
- Melted butter (4 Tbsp.)
- Crushed garlic cloves (4)
- Diced shallots (2)

Ginger Dressing
- Olive oil (4 Tbsp.)
- Brown sugar
- Minced garlic cloves (2)
- Ginger (1 Tbsp.)
- Balsamic vinegar (2 Tbsp.)

Preparations:
1. To start this recipe, bring out the sous vide machine and fill it up with some water. Set the temperature to 183 degrees.
2. Take out enough bags so that you can place each of the vegetables into their own food safe bag. Divide the seasonings, butter, and garlic between these bags.
3. Seal up the bags properly, making sure that you get rid of all the air that is inside. Place

into the warm water bath and cook these for 40 minutes.

4. After the vegetables are done cooking, take the bag with the tomatoes out and continue cooking the other bags.

5. When this time is up, take the bags with the peppers and zucchini out. Set the timer for another 55 minutes to finish up with the shallots.

6. After this time, all the vegetables should be done. Chop up the ingredients and toss them in a serving bowl. Set this to the side.

7. Meanwhile, mix together the balsamic vinegar, ginger, minced garlic cloves, brown sugar, and olive oil. Drizzle this on top of the prepared vegetables and then serve.

Bean Salad

Ingredients:

- Sugar (.5 c.)
- White vinegar (.5 c.)
- Olive oil (.5 c.)
- Diced red bell pepper (1)
- Diced sweet onion (1)
- Cooked chickpeas (2 c.)
- Cooked kidney beans (2 c.)
- Trimmed green beans (1 lb.)
- Parsley (1 Tbsp.)
- Pepper (.5 tsp.)
- Salt (1 tsp.)

Preparations:

1. Fill up your sous vide machine and set the temperature to 183 degrees. Place your green bean into a food safe bag and seal it up.
2. Place the bag of vegetables into the water bath and cook it for an hour.
3. After this time, remove your vegetables from the water bath and let them chill.
4. Drain out the green beans before cutting in half and place into a large bowl. Add the bell peppers, onion, chickpeas, and kidney beans.
5. You can make your vinaigrette by combining the parsley, pepper, salt, sugar, vinegar, and oil. Pour this over the salad and then stir until it is all coated.
6. Keep this salad inside the fridge until you are ready to serve.

Blueberry Vinaigrette

Ingredients:

- Dijon mustard (1 Tbsp.)
- Balsamic vinegar (1 Tbsp.)
- White wine vinegar (3 Tbsp.)
- Grape seed oil (.3 c.)
- Granulated sugar (1 tsp.)
- Blueberries (1 pint)

Preparations:

1. For this recipe, take out the sous vide machine and fill it up with water. Set the water bath to warm up to 150 degrees.
2. Place your blueberries into a food safe bag and then seal it all up. Make sure that you are not stacking the blueberries.
3. Place this bag of blueberries into your water bath and cook for 40 minutes. After this time, take the blueberries out and give them some time to cool down.
4. Use a blender and add all of the ingredients inside. Blend until this becomes emulsified and smooth.

Thai Mango Salad

Ingredients:

- Red Thai chilies (3)
- Minced garlic cloves (1)
- Dark brown sugar (3 Tbsp.)
- Salt
- Peanut oil (1 tsp.)
- Lime juice (3 Tbsp.)
- Green beans (2 oz.)
- Green mangos (2)
- Cherry tomatoes (5)
- Toasted peanuts (2 Tbsp.)
- Thai basil leaves (2 Tbsp.)
- Chopped cilantro (1 Tbsp.)

Preparations:

1. Start this recipe out by slicing the beans a bit and then peel and slice the mango.
2. Bring out your sous vide machine and fill it up with some water. Heat up the water bath to 149 degrees.
3. Fill the food safe bag with mango, green beans, some salt, and pepper. Place into the water bath for ten minutes.
4. Use a pestle and mortar to prepare the salad. Pound together the chilies, garlic, and sugar together for 30 seconds and then pour the juice into a bowl with the mango and green beans.
5. Pound this gently and combine with some basil and tomatoes.
6. Toss everything together and enjoy.

Broccoli Salad

Ingredients:
- Broccoli florets (4 heads)
- Cherry tomatoes (12)
- Salt
- Pepper
- Olive oil (6 Tbsp.)
- Tuscan olives (10)

Preparations:
1. Take out your sous vide machine and let the water heat up to 183 degrees.
2. While the sous vide water bath is heating up, combine the salt, pepper, broccoli, and half the oil together and mix to coat.
3. Add this mixture into a food safe bag and then seal it shut properly. Place the bag into the water bath and let them cook for the next 45 minutes.
4. While that is cooking, quarter the tomatoes and place them on a platter with the olives.
5. When the broccoli mixture is done cooking, drain away the liquid and place it on the container with the other ingredients. Sprinkle some pepper and salt before serving.

Chapter 5: Dinner Ideas the Whole Family Will Love

Quiche Lorraine

Ingredients:
- Puff pastry (1 sheet
- Pepper (1 tsp.)
- Salt (.5 tsp.)
- Nutmeg
- Chives (2 Tbsp.)
- Plain Greek yogurt (.5 c.)
- Shredded Gruyere cheese (4 oz.)
- Eggs (3)

Preparations:
1. Take out a biscuit cutter and cut up your pastry sheet into rounds. Bake these in the oven based on the instructions on the package.
2. Take out your sous vide machine and let the water bath heat up to 165 degrees.
3. While that is heating up, beat the eggs together before adding in the pepper, salt, nutmeg, chives, and yogurt. Stir the cheese as well.
4. When this is ready, take out a food safe bag and pour the egg mixture inside.
5. Place this bag into the water bath and let the whole dish cook for the next twenty minutes. Take the bag out after this time and let it cool down.

6. Take the egg out of the bag and place on a cutting board. Use that biscuit cutter again and cut rounds out of the egg.

7. One of these egg rounds should go on each pastry that you cooked earlier and then sprinkle with chives.

French Omelette

Ingredients:

- Parsley (.25 Tbsp.)
- Minced chives (.25 Tbsp.)
- Melted butter (1 Tbsp.)
- Eggs (3)
- Pepper (.25 tsp.)
- Salt (.25 tsp.)
- Plain Greek yogurt (1 Tbsp.)
- Minced rosemary (.25 tsp.)
- Minced tarragon (.25 Tbsp.)

Preparations:

1. To start this recipe, bring out your sous vide machine and heat up the water bath to 165 degrees.
2. While that is heating up, beat together the yogurt, butter, and eggs. Then you can add the pepper, salt, and herbs as well.
3. Pour this mixture into your food safe bag and then seal it up so all the air is gone. Place the bag into the water bath.
4. This dish needs to cook for about 10 minutes. At this time, take the eggs out of the water bath and nicely press them into the shape of an omelet.
5. Put the bag back into the water bath and let it cook for another ten minutes.
6. After this time, take the omelet out and put it on a plate. Garnish with the parsley before serving.

Summer Ratatouille

Ingredients:

- Sliced zucchini (2)
- Crushed tomatoes, canned (4)
- Pepper (1 tsp.)
- Salt (.5 tsp.)
- Olive oil (2 Tbsp.)
- Basil (6 sprigs)
- Minced garlic cloves (6)
- Sliced Spanish onion (.5)
- Sliced eggplants (2)
- Sliced bell peppers (2)
- Bread for serving
- Parmesan cheese

Preparations:

1. Take out your sous vide machine and fill it with water. Let the water bath heat up to 185 degrees.
2. While the sous vide machine is heating up, combine the pepper, salt, olive oil, basil, garlic, onion, eggplant, bell peppers, zucchini, and tomatoes into a food safe bag.
3. Make sure that all of the air is out of the bag before sealing it up and placing it into the water bath. Let these vegetables cook for the next two hours.
4. Pour the ratatouille into a bowl and garnish with olive oil, Parmesan, and basil before serving with the bread.

Cauliflower Alfredo

Ingredients:
- Pepper
- Salt
- Vegetable stock (.5 c.)
- Butter (2 Tbsp.)
- Milk (2 Tbsp.)
- Chopped cauliflower florets (2 c.)
- Garlic cloves (2)

Preparations:
1. For this recipe, take out the sous vide machine and fill it up with water. Let the water bath heat up to 181 degrees.
2. Place all of your ingredients inside of a food safe bag and seal it up without any air inside.
3. Add the bag into your sous vide water bath and let it cook for about two hours.
4. When the meal is done, take it out of the water bath and let it cool down for a bit.
5. Bring out a blender or the food processor and blend it until smooth. Season and then serve.

Eggplant Lasagna

Ingredients:

- Salt (2 tsp.)
- Tomato sauce (1.5 c.)
- Eggplants (2 lbs.)
- Sliced mozzarella (4 oz.)
- Italian cheese blend (4 oz.)
- Chopped basil (.25 c.)
- Seasoned breadcrumbs (1 Tbsp.)
- Parmesan cheese (2 oz.)

Preparations:

1. Take out your sous vide machine and then add in water to the right lines. Heat up this water bath and let it heat up to 183 degrees.

2. Take your eggplant and get rid of all the peel. Slice into thin rounds and sprinkle with some salt. Allow these to drain for 30 minutes while drying.

3. Add half of your sauce with a layer of eggplant into your food safe bag. Top this with the mozzarella cheese and some of the grated blend.

4. Now add a bit of the parmesan cheese before topping with the basil, another row of eggplant, and more sauce.

5. When all of these ingredients are in the bag, seal it up without any air inside and then place into a water bath.

6. Cook the meal for about three hours. When the time is done, clip the corner of your bag to

keep the juices inside. Slid your eggplant to a serving platter and let it cool down a bit.

7. When the dish is ready, pour the rest of the sauce, the bread crumbs, and the rest of your cheese options. Enjoy this over some pasta and enjoy.

Squash Casserole

Ingredients:

- Eggs (2)
- Salt
- Pepper
- Summer squash (1.5 lbs.)
- Chopped onion (.75 c.)
- Butter (2 Tbsp.)
- Whole milk (.5 c.)
- Potato chips, crumbled (.5 c.)

Preparations:

1. Quarter the squash going lengthwise and then slice into .25-inches thick.
2. Now you can prepare your sous vide water bath by bringing out your machine and letting it heat up to 176 degrees.
3. Take out four mason jars and grease with a little butter. In a skillet, melt the butter and add some onions to cook for a few minutes.
4. Toss the salt and some zucchini in as well and cook for another ten minutes.
5. Blend the summer squash to each of your jars and let them cool down a bit.
6. Whip together the eggs and milk with some salt and pepper before adding to the jars as well.
7. Close the lids up and set them into the warm water bath for an hour.

Once your timer goes off, arrange the jars on a cooling rack for a bit and then garnish with some chips before serving.

Thanksgiving Squash

Ingredients:
- Salt
- Pepper
- Red kidney beans (1 can)
- Garlic cloves (3)
- Olive oil (2 Tbsp.)
- Sliced winter squash (1)
- Diced tomatoes (1 can)
- Coriander (.5 tsp.)
- Cumin powder (.25 tsp.)
- Hot paprika (1 tsp.)

Preparations:
1. For this recipe, bring out your sous vide machine and fill it up with some water. Let the hot water bath reach 175 degrees.
2. Take out a food safe bag and fill it up with the squash. Place this into the water bath so that it can cook for 50 minutes.
3. When the cooking time is almost up, take out a pan and heat up some olive oil. Cook the garlic until it becomes aromatic.
4. Stir the rest of the ingredients, including the squash for about 5 minutes, check to see if the beans are done. Serve this warm.

Spicy and Saucy Tofu

Ingredients:
- Ketjap Manis (1 Tbsp.)
- Minced garlic cloves (4)
- Hot sauce (1 tsp.)
- Vegetable broth (1.5 c.)
- Cubed tofu (.5 lb.)
- Onion powder (.5 tsp.)
- Clove (.5 tsp.)
- Apple cider vinegar (1 Tbsp.)
- Molasses (1 Tbsp.)

Preparations:
1. To start, you should bring out the sous vide machine and turn it on so the water bath can heat up to 183 degrees.
2. Bring out a mixing dish and combine the onion powder, clove, vinegar, molasses, Ketjap manis, hot sauce, garlic, and broth until it is well mixed.
3. Add this mixture into a food safe bag before adding the cubes of tofu. Make sure to seal this bag up properly.
4. Place the bag into the warm water bath and let it cook for an hour and fifteen minutes.
5. When this is done, allow the tofu some time to cool down before serving with a fresh salad.

Veggie Delight Meal

Ingredients:
- Sliced leek (1)
- Sliced eggplant (1)
- Sliced sweet peppers (3)
- Sliced zucchinis (2)
- Sliced Roma tomatoes (2)
- Sesame seeds (1 Tbsp.)
- Italian parsley (1 Tbsp.)
- Hot sauce (.25 tsp.)
- Tomato ketchup (2 Tbsp.)
- Peanut oil (.5 c.)
- Garlic head (1)
- Peppercorns (.5 tsp.)
- Cayenne pepper (1 tsp.)
- Salt (1 tsp.)

Preparations:
1. Bring out the sous vide machine and let the water bath heat up to 183 degrees.
2. Take each of your vegetables and place them into their own separate food safe bag. Season each bag with the green peppercorns, cayenne pepper, and salt.
3. Divide the garlic and the oil into each bag as well and then vacuum seal them closed.
4. When the water is ready, lower each of these bags into the water bath, making sure that they are submerged properly.

5. Allow these vegetables to cook in the water bath for the next 35 minutes. After that time is up, take the bag with the tomatoes out and set to the side.

6. Cook the rest of the bags for another 35 minutes and then take the bags with the sweet peppers and zucchini out.

7. Set the timer one more time to cook for another 30 minutes so the leeks and eggplant can finish up.

8. After this time, chop the vegetables before tossing them in a bowl with the hot sauce and ketchup. Serve with the sesame seeds and parsley on top and enjoy.

Vegan Pilaf

Ingredients:
- Smashed garlic cloves (3)
- Chopped white onion (1)
- Broccoli head (1)
- Chopped carrots (2)
- Salt
- Pepper
- Bouillon cubes (2)
- Paprika (.5 tsp.)
- Cumin powder (.25 tsp.)
- Water (3.5 c.)
- Arborio rice (1.5 c.)
- Olive oil (1 Tbsp.)
- Rosemary (1 tsp.)
- Marjoram (1 tsp.)

Preparations:
1. Take out your sous vide machine and let the water bath heat up to 183 degrees.
2. Each of your vegetables should go into a different food safe bag. Divide your olive oil, rosemary, marjoram, and garlic between these bags.
3. Turn the timer of your sous vide machine to 30 minutes and place the bags into the water bath. Take the broccoli and the onion out of the water at this time.

4. Bring out another bag and add the rice, bouillon cubes, paprika, cumin powder, and water to it.

5. Place these into the water bath and let them cook for the next 45 minutes.

6. After this time, check to see if the rice is done. If it is, combine it in a bowl with your prepared vegetables and add some pepper and salt before serving.

Pear and Squash Dinner

Ingredients:

- Peeled and diced Vidalia onion (1)
- Diced Bartlett pears (2)
- Diced summer squash (1)
- Vegetable broth (1.5 c.)
- Minced coriander (.5 tsp.)
- Allspice (.5 tsp.)
- Minced ginger root (1 tsp.)
- White pepper
- Salt
- Oregano (2 sprigs)
- *Vegan Crème Fraiche*
- Agave nectar (1 Tbsp.)
- Sesame oil (.5 c.)
- Lime juice (1 tsp.)
- Soymilk (.5 c.)

Preparations:

1. Take out the sous vide machine and fill it up with some water. Let the water bath heat up to 183 degrees.
2. Add your white pepper, salt, oregano, onion, pears, squash in a food safe bag and vacuum seal them closed.
3. Place the bag of food into the water bath and let it cook for 55 minutes.
4. While this meal is cooking, you can work on the vegan cream. Take out your blender and mix together the lime juice and soymilk. Place to the side.

5. Pulse together the agave nectar and sesame oil and then pour this one into the soymilk mixture, mix it until thick.

6. When the vegetables are done, move them over to a pot. Stir the prepared cream, broth, coriander, allspice, and ginger. Let this warm up a bit.

7. Take out your immersion hand blender and blend this mixture until it becomes as creamy as you would like. You can choose to chill this mixture or serve it at room temperature.

Mediterranean Vegetable Skillet

Ingredients:
- Minced jalapeno pepper (1)
- Sliced parsnip (1)
- Sliced carrots (2)
- Cubed Yukon gold potatoes (.5 lb.)
- Slivered almonds (2 Tbsp.)
- Garbanzo beans (1 can)
- Chopped tomato (1)
- Chopped sage (1 Tbsp.)
- Chopped basil (1 Tbsp.)
- Minced garlic cloves (4)
- Chopped purple onion (1)
- Olive oil (1.5 Tbsp.)
- Oregano (1 sprig)
- Rosemary (2 sprigs)
- Thyme (1 sprig)
- Peanut oil (1 Tbsp.)
- Pepper
- Salt

Preparations:
1. Take out the sous vide machine and fill it up with water. Let this water bath heat up to 185 degrees.
2. Take each of the vegetables and add them to a separate food safe bag. Then divide the oregano, rosemary, thyme, peanut oil, pepper, salt, and jalapeno pepper to each bag.

3. Arrange a rack into your sous vide machine and then lower the bags of food inside. Let these cook for about 90 minutes.

4. Warm some oil in a skillet and cook the garlic and onion until they become tender. Stir the tomato, sage, and basil and cook until heated through.

5. Now add in the cooked vegetables and the garbanzo beans. Take the skillet from the heat and adjust the seasonings.

6. Garnish this dish with the almond slivers and enjoy.

Pasta Casserole Recipe

Ingredients:

- Mint (.25 c.)
- Feta cheese (.25 c.)
- Kalamata olives
- Sliced almonds (.66 c.)
- Salt (.5 tsp.)
- Greek yogurt (2 c.)
- Kale (3 handfuls)
- Butternut squash (1.5 c.)
- Whole wheat pasta (8 oz.)
- Lemon (1)

Preparations:

1. Take out the sous vide machine. Let the water bath heat up to 165 degrees.
1. Add a bit of water and the whole wheat pasta to a food safe bag and place into the water bath. Let this cook for about an hour.
2. When the pasta is done, drain out the water and set it aside in a bowl. In a second bowl, combine the salt, yogurt, and garlic together.
3. Pour this on top of the noodles and add the squash and kale as well. Add half of the almonds on top and sprinkle with some feta and olive oil.
4. Turn the oven to 400 degrees. Place the dish into the oven. After 25 minutes, take it out. Top with the mint and almonds and enjoy.

Tempeh Curry

Ingredients:

- Turmeric (.25 tsp.)
- Curry powder (1 tsp.)
- Cumin seeds (1 tsp.)
- Yellow onion (1)
- Olive oil (2 Tbsp.)
- Butter (1 Tbsp.)
- Cilantro
- Tempeh (8 oz.)
- Salt (2 tsp.)
- Potatoes (1.5 lbs.)
- Dollop of cream
- Water (.75 c)
- Diced tomatoes (1 c.)
- Cayenne pepper (.5 tsp.)

Preparations:

1. Take out the sous vide machine and fill it up with water. Let the water bath heat up to 183 degrees.
2. Take out some food safe bags and add the potatoes inside. When the water is warm, add these inside and let the potatoes cook for 90 minutes.
3. When the potatoes are done, take them out of the water and out of the bag. Bring out a skillet and melt the butter.
4. Add the onion, curry powder, turmeric, and cumin seeds and cook for a short time.
5. Add the water, salt, and tomatoes and the tempeh. Let this simmer for five minutes before adding the potatoes.
6. Sprinkle with some cilantro and enjoy.

Avocado Spring Rolls

Ingredients:
- Rice paper wrappers (8)
- Sliced avocado (1)
- Tofu (6 oz.)
- Cooked rice (1 c.)
- Chopped hazelnuts (.25 c.)
- Salt (.25 tsp.)
- Garlic clove (.25 c.)
- Oregano (.25 c.)
- Olive oil (.5 c.)

Preparations:
1. Take out your sous vide machine and fill it with water. You will need the water bath to heat up to 185 degrees.
2. While that is heating up, take out two food safe bags. One needs to hold the avocado and one to the rice with a bit of water inside.
3. Add the bag with the rice into the water bath and let it cook for 45 minutes. After this time, add the avocado and cook for another 45 minutes.
4. While that is cooking, make your oregano paste, mix together the parsley, salt, garlic, oregano, and olive oil and cook until it is smooth.
5. When the rice and avocado are done, mix them together in a bowl with the rest of the ingredients.
6. Lay out the rice paper wrappers and dip each one in some hot water for 3 seconds.
7. Place on a surface and then put a bit of the mixture into each one. Wrap these and then serve with the horseradish sauce.

Avocado Cucumber and Sweet Potatoes

Ingredients:

- Cubed sweet potato (1)
- Toasted sesame seeds (2 Tbsp.)
- Sliced cucumber (1)
- Nori sheets (23)
- Agave (2 tsp.)
- Lemon juice (1)
- Brown rice (2 c.)

Preparations:

1. The first thing that you should do is take out your sous vide machine and let the water heat up to about 200 degrees.
2. Take out a food safe bag and fill it with the rice and a bit of water. Add this to the sous vide water bath and then cook for 90 minutes.
3. When the rice is done, take it out of your water bath and let it cool down. Pour into a bowl and add the agave and lemon juice. Let this cook together for another hour.
4. To work on the right side of the make, take out a bamboo mat and place the nori over it. When the rice is done, place some rice in the middle.
5. Line up the rice, cucumber, and avocado over it and then roll up the nori sheet upwards.
6. Place this in the fridge to let it chill until you are ready to serve.
7. Now you can work on the nigiri, chill the sweet potatoes and then mold the rest of the rice into a prism and chill. When you are ready, serve both of these together.

Five-Veg Lasagna

Ingredients:
- Chopped mushrooms (15)
- Sliced aborigine (1)
- Olive oil (2 Tbsp.)
- Pine nuts
- Parmesan style cheese
- Ricotta (250 gm.)
- Frozen spinach (1 can)
- Lasagna sheets (10)
- Chopped and roasted red peppers (2)

Preparations:
1. To start this one, take out the sous vide machine and fill it up with water. Let the water bath heat up to 185 degrees.
2. While the water bath is heating up, you can bring out some food safe bags. Place the noodles inside and then add to the water bath.
3. These noodles need to cook in the hot water bath for about an hour so they can become soft. Let them cool down a bit before serving.
4. Turn on the oven to 360 degrees. While this is heating up, you can take out a pan and fry the aborigine and olive oil for five minutes.
5. When this is soft, move it over to a boil and then fry the mushrooms and the rest of the oil for a bit. Add this and the peppers to the aborigine.

6. Take out a pan and layer the vegetable mixture and the lasagna sheets. Mix together the ricotta, spinach, and half of the Parmesan cheese and then spoon this over the rest of the dish.
7. Sprinkle with the rest of the cheese and the pine nuts on top. Cover with some foil and place into the oven.
8. After twenty minutes, take the lasagna out of the oven and then serve with a salad.

Stuffed Potatoes

Ingredients:
- Sweet corn (100 g)
- Grated Cheddar cheese (1 c.)
- Potatoes (5)
- Diced mixed peppers (.5 c.)
- Herb mixture

Preparations:
1. For this recipe, take out your sous vide machine and fill it up with water. Let this water bath heat up to 200 degrees.
2. Bring out your food safe bags. Place the potatoes inside of your bags and then into the water bath. Let these cook for two hours.
3. When the cooking process is done, take the potatoes out and let them cool down a bit.
4. Turn on the oven to 400 degrees. When the potatoes are cooled down, cut them into halves and then spoon out the middle of each of them.
5. Place the insides of the potatoes into a bowl and add the sweet corns, peppers, and cheese.
6. Mix all of this together well and then place the mixture back into the skins of the potatoes.
7. Place all of this into the baking dish and cook for a few minutes to make it golden brown before serving.

Cheesy Veg Burgers

Ingredients:
- Grated Cheddar cheese (.5 c.)
- Beans (1 can)
- Soy sauce (2 Tbsp.)
- Seasoning (1 Tbsp.)
- Chopped carrots (2)
- Mushrooms (200 g.)
- Leeks (2)
- Olive oil (2 Tbsp.)
- Granary bread (4 slices)
- Tomatoes
- Lettuce
- Burger bun

Preparations:
1. Take out your sous vide machine and fill it up with some water. Heat up your water bath to 185 degrees.
2. Place your mushrooms, beans, carrots, and leeks into a food safe bag and seal it up properly.
3. Add this bag of food into the warm water bath and let it cook for 90 minutes.
4. Now heat up some oil in a pan and then add the cooked vegetables along with the soy sauce and the seasonings.
5. After a few minutes, place these vegetables along with the bread, cheese, and beans in the

food processors and work until it becomes a thick paste.

6. Shape this paste into a burger patty and then chill it for a bit in the fridge.

7. After a half hour or so, add a bit more oil into a pan and let each side of your burger cook for 3 minutes to make it crispy.

8. Lay out the burger bun and then add the lettuce, tomatoes, and other toppings of your choice on top before serving.

Chapter 6: Vegetarian Desserts

Apple Crisp

Ingredients:
- Salt (.5 tsp.)
- Cinnamon (.5 tsp.)
- Flour (.75 c.)
- Rolled oats (1 c.)
- Butter (.5 c.)
- Lemon juice (1 tsp.)
- Brown sugar (1.25 c.)
- Diced apples (2 c.)

Preparations:
1. Take out the sous vide machine and set it so the water bath reaches 183 degrees.
2. Place the lemon juice, .25 cup of brown sugar, and apples inside of a food safe bag and seal it shut.
3. Place this apple mixture into the water bath and cook it for about an hour.
4. When the cooking time is almost done, turn the oven on so it heats up to 350 degrees.
5. Inside a big bowl, cut the butter with the salt, cinnamon, flour, rolled oats and the rest of the brown sugar.
6. Spread this mixture on the baking sheet and then place into the oven. After fifteen minutes are done, take it out and allow some time to cool.
7. When you are ready to serve, spoon some of the apple mixture onto a plate and then top with the oat mixture. You can add some vanilla ice cream if you would like as well.

Spiced Pumpkin Puree

Ingredients:
- Butter (.25 c.)
- Salt (.5 tsp.)
- Ground cloves (.25 tsp.)
- Cardamom (.25 tsp.)
- Nutmeg (.5 tsp.)
- Ginger (1 tsp.)
- Cinnamon (1.5 tsp.)
- Brown sugar (.75 c.)
- Sugar pumpkin (4 lbs.)

Preparations:
1. Cut the pumpkin so it is in quarters. Scoop the seeds out from the inner part and then get rid of it. Peel and cut off the outer skins and then slice the pumpkin so you end up with smaller wedges.
2. Take out your sous vide machine and set it so the water bath reaches 183 degrees.
3. In a small bowl, mix the spices and the brown sugar. Place the pumpkin into a food safe bag and sprinkle the sugar and spice mixture on top.
4. Cut your butter into smaller cubes and add to the bag, making sure the pumpkin is nice and flat. Seal the bag shut.
5. Place your bag into the water bath and let it cook for three hours.
6. Once done, take the bag out of the water bath and pour all of the ingredients into a bowl.
7. Using a hand blender or potato masher, puree the pumpkin. This dish works well as a side dish or pie filling.

Peaches and Brandy

Ingredients:
- Halved peaches (4)
- Cognac (.3 c.)
- Sugar (.5 c.)
- Water (.5 c.)

Preparations:
1. Take out a pan and heat up the sugar and water, taking the time to stir often. When the sugar has dissolved, remove from the heat and let it cool.
2. Stir your brandy and cognac inside and then set the syrup aside.
3. Take out your sous vide machine and let the water bath heat up to 183 degrees.
4. Place the peach halves into the food safe bag and seal it shut properly. Make sure that your peaches are in one layer rather than stacked.
5. Place your peaches into the water bath and cook them for 45 minutes.
6. When the peaches are done cooking, remove them from the water bath and let them chill in an ice bath for a bit.
7. Peel off the skin and then slice the peaches before you serve with some vanilla ice cream.

Strawberries and Grand Marnier

Ingredients:

- Mint (2 Tbsp.)
- Orange zest (.5 tsp.)
- Grand Marnier (2 Tbsp.)
- Granulated sugar (.25 c.)
- Sliced strawberries (3 c.)
- Optional vanilla ice cream

Preparations:

1. Fill up your sous vide machine with water and set the temperature of the water bath to 183 degrees.
2. Take out a food safe bag and combine the orange zest, Grand Marnier, sugar, and strawberries inside. Seal it tight.
3. Place your strawberry mixture into the water bath and let it cook for about 15 minutes.
4. After this time, take the mixture out of the bath and then place some ice to help with the chilling process.
5. Spoon these strawberries and syrup into some serving bowls before topping with mint. Serve with the vanilla ice cream.

Pistachio and Mango Rice Pudding

Ingredients:
- Dried mango, diced (.5 c.)
- Cooked white rice (2 c.)
- Vanilla (1 tsp.)
- Granulated sugar (.5 c.)
- Eggs (3)
- Heavy cream (.66 c.)
- Whole milk (.3 c.)
- Chopped pistachios (.5 c.)

Preparations:
1. Fill up your water bath with some water. Make sure that the water bath reaches 183 degrees.
2. Take out a bowl and whisk together the vanilla, sugar, eggs, cream, and milk. When these are combined, stir the dried mango and the rice.
3. Pour this whole mixture into your food safe bag and then seal it shut without any air inside.
4. Place this bag of food into the water bath and let it cook for the next 40 minutes.
5. When this is done, spoon the mixture into a serving bowl and top with the pistachios. Serve it either warm or chilled.

Pecan and Raisin Rice Pudding

Ingredients:
- Rum (1 Tbsp.)
- Vanilla (1 tsp.)
- Granulated sugar (.5 c.)
- Eggs (3)
- Heavy cream (.66 c.)
- Whole milk (1.3 c.)
- Chopped pecans (.5 c.)
- Raisins (.5 c.)
- White rice, cooked (2 c.)

Preparations:
1. Take out your sous vide machine and fill it up with some water. Let the water bath heat up to 183 degrees.
2. While the water bath is heating up, bring out a bowl and add the rum, vanilla, raisins, rice, sugar, eggs, cream, and milk.
3. When this mixture is ready, pour the mixture into a food safe bag and seal it up properly.
4. Place this whole mixture into the water bath and cook it for about 40 minutes. Allow the mixture some time to cool down before serving with the toasted pecans on top.

Figgy Pudding

Ingredients:

- Chopped figs, dried (1 c.)
- Melted butter (1 stick)
- Eggs (3)
- Nutmeg (.5 tsp.)
- Cinnamon (1 tsp.)
- Baking powder (2 tsp.)
- Sugar (1 c.)
- Bread crumbs (1 c.)
- Flour (1.5 c.)
- Brandy (1 c.)

Preparations:

1. Soak your figs in the brandy overnight. When this recipe is ready, get rid of all but .25 cup of the brandy.
2. Take out the sous vide machine and fill it up. Let the water bath heat up to 195 degrees.
3. While the water bath is heating up, combine the nutmeg, cinnamon, baking powder, bread crumbs, and flour in a bowl.
4. In a second bowl, beat the eggs slowly before adding the figs with brandy, the butter, and the sugar.
5. Slowly add in the flour mixture to this second bowl and mix to combine.
6. Pour this batter into some mason jars and then put the lids on tight. Place the jars into the water bath and let them cook for 6 hours.
7. When this is done, let the pudding cool down a bit before inverting onto a plate and serving warm.

Banoffee Pie

Ingredients:

- Graham cracker crust (1)
- Sliced bananas (6)
- Brown sugar (.5 c.)
- Butter (.25 c.)
- Condensed milk, sweetened (1 can)
- Whipped cream

Preparations:

1. Take out the sous vide machine and fill it with water. Let the water bath heat up to 185 degrees.
2. While the water bath is heating up, stir together the sugar, butter, and condensed milk. Pour this into your mason jar and screw the lid nice and tight.
3. Add the jar into the prepared water bath and cook for the next 20 hours so the toffee becomes thick.
4. When the toffee is done, it is time to prepare the pie. Take out your crust and spread out a layer of the bananas on the bottom.
5. Pour the prepared toffee over this, then spread out another layer of the bananas, followed by more toffee.
6. Continue this until you use up all the ingredients. Top with some whipped cream and then serve.

Lemon Curd Pie

Ingredients:

- Pie crust, prepared (1)
- Sugar (1 c.)
- Egg yolks (6)
- Juice from lemons (4)
- Melted butter (.25 c.)
- Whipped cream for serving

Preparations:

1. Take out your sous vide machine and fill it up with water. Let this water bath heat up to 180 degrees.

2. Whisk together the lemon juice, butter, and sugar. Then add the egg yolks and whisk well.

3. Pour this mixture into a bag and seal it up properly. Place the bag into your prepared water bath and then let it cook for the next 45 minutes.

4. Take out your pie crust and get it all set up. When the bag of food is done, pour the curd into the crust.

5. Cover everything with some plastic wrap and then transfer to the fridge to cool overnight before serving.

Conclusion

Thanks for making it through to the end of this book, let's hope it was informative and able to provide you with all of the tools you need to achieve your goals whatever they may be.

The next step is to give a few of these recipes a try. If you are looking to stay on the vegetarian diet but you want to be able to create some delicious meals that are easy to finish, this book is going to help you get this done. Not only will you be able to use some of the great cooking techniques that many people are falling in love with, but you can follow this healthy lifestyle choice as well.

This book will provide you all of the information that you need to get started. We took some time to talk about the vegetarian diet and some of the basics that come with that diet plan as well as some of the basics of the vegetarian diet for those that are considering using it for their health and weight loss goals. Once those topics are done, it is time to move on to some of the best recipes that you can try using the sous vide cooking method while sticking with the requirements of the vegetarian diet.

When you are ready to try out the sous vide cooking method but you need to watch out for some of the meat recipes that are so popular, make sure to check out this book and learn how to make some of these delicious recipes.

Finally, if you found this book useful in any way, a review on Amazon is always appreciated!

Made in the USA
Las Vegas, NV
21 August 2021

28576193R00046